I0169004

Ten Thousand Spiderwebs Bright with Dew

Ten Thousand Spiderwebs Bright with Dew

Poems by

Lynne Santy Tanner

© 2022 Lynne Santy Tanner. All rights reserved.
This material may not be reproduced in any form, published,
reprinted, recorded, performed, broadcast,
rewritten or redistributed without
the explicit permission of Lynne Santy Tanner.
All such actions are strictly prohibited by law.

Cover design by Shay Culligan
Cover art "The High Meadow" by Lynne Santy Tanner

ISBN: 978-1-63980-120-6

Kelsay Books
502 South 1040 East, A-119
American Fork, Utah 84003
Kelsaybooks.com

In memory of Mike

and

with gratitude to The Chapin School

We gather together to ask the Lord's blessing

Acknowledgments

I am grateful to the editors of the publications in which the following poems first appeared, some in a slightly different form.

Kakalak 2016: "Eight Dyslexic Kids Before Dyslexia Had a Name"

Kakalak 2017: "The Japanese Cherry"

Kakalak 2018: "The Voice of the Turtle is Heard in Our Land," "Already Half a Century"

Kakalak 2020: "An Abiding Image"

Hermit Feathers Review: "A Morning Lesson," "After the Ball," "An Aubade"

QuillsEdge Press 50/50 Poems & Translations by Womxn over 50: "The Song of the Mocking Bird," "Midsummer," "On This Bright Day"

I thank Elizabeth Nields who walks with me through these poems, Nancy Womack and Kathy Ackerman for the arms that are always around me, and Lucy Hooper without whom I can do nothing.

I thank Cathy Smith Bowers for the title *"An Abiding Image."*

Contents

A Sweet Scent Rising

The Voice of the Turtle Is Heard in Our Land

A narrow beam of sun breaks through a roiling sky,
presses bare white trees against Prussian blue mountains
and spotlights Chimney Rock.

Clouds billow into the gorge.
A green thicket of pine appears,
then disappears in the bluster.

Today, February second, first day of Druid spring,
Candlemas, the day Christ was presented at the Temple,
Simeon proclaiming, "Mine eyes have seen Thy salvation."

Yesterday and this morning, the sound of the turtledove.
Surely, if I open the door and step outside,
I will hear the angels sing.

Buckets of Yellow

One whiff
of February Golds
on my kitchen table

and I am in New York
where the sun is shining
on Madison Avenue

where once
jonquils and tulips were sold
from horse-drawn drays.

When one appeared
outside our second grade classroom,

Miss Cronk stopped everything,
said, "Quickly, children
take your crayons
to the window,
draw the flowers."

The wagons are gone
but in March and April
greengrocers still
put buckets of yellow daffodils
on the sidewalks

their sweet scent rising.

A Morning Lesson

....with that song and what I have found in books,
maybe the secret could be learned . . .
—Loren Eiseley

His sermon opens the morning
with phrases precise and pious.
He preaches from bare branch

his buff breast streaked with brown
a glowing chasuble in the sun.

Finished, he drops to the ground
to peck a stray seed
then retires to dewy leaves—
no further lessons.

But soon the mockingbird,
not so handsome as the Brown Thrasher,
rolls out *his* recitative,
words bright and clear,

chitter-chitter, click-click, pretty-bird, pretty-bird.
Once, twice and still again, he loops calls
from all the neighborhood,

even the *brrrr* of a lawn mower.

An Abiding Image

A June morning,
        dew drenched,
the lawn iridescent green:

a small girl,
        in soft cotton gown
and a red cowboy hat

walks up the hill
        toward me,
her bare feet marking

a trail through wet grass.

Years later
        I sit on that hill,

the morning sky
        patterned with a lace of new leaves.

The cat and I survey
        our peaceable kingdom.

But only I
        see the slash of red

and a bruised path in the grass.

Midsummer

The days of June
seem longer than ever I remember,
the sky so late
fading from pink to pearl,
still aglow after ten o'clock.

I am a child again going to bed by day,
and up at dawn.
Clear morning air
carries me all the way to blazing afternoon.

In my garden
orange daylilies dance
arm and arm with purple iris large as salad plates
and bee balm sways beside bold rudbeckia.

Along the highway sumac flames
and the blinding sun
turns our dining room to gold
each evening.

Now by decree
it may go no farther,
but must retrace its steps
across four mountain tops
as I begin to count the days.

The Song of the Mocking Bird

Before leaving to visit Suzanne, I walk my road
as though I'll be gone years instead of days.

The Hawk is scolding loud above David's land.
David has been cutting pines all week
but the Hawk is angry with the Crow.

Higher up the road I hear the Mocking Bird,
a good sign, then a "Georgia Bird"
        as my brother Chris
called the Blue Jay when we were young
           and visiting our Grandmother.

The Cardinal is silent this morning
though not hidden
as he weaves his red thread through the scrub
between Mark's house and the house of that new Neighbor

who is again working in his yard,
never stopping to listen.

And if the song goes on much longer
I will be late getting on my way
and have no time to write this down.

Trespassing

The Hamlin farm stretches below me,
minute black cows meandering fields
laced with random fencing.

For days, morning and evening,
the tractor, like a flame that burns
but does not consume,

cut   then mounded the hay
into neat rows.

Today it sings a new song as it loads bales
onto the conveyor belt to the loft.

Kenny doesn't know I stand day after day
on this high hill asking, What is it I cannot name
that breaks my heart
                    and heals it?

This Bright Day

Yesterday, searching for my work shoes
in Elizabeth's far barn,
I discovered a tumble of mice under a blanket.

They looked at me with such terror
I closed the wardrobe and left them
but today,
      Elizabeth and I are going after them
with a bucket . . . Once they're in it,
they can't crawl out, she says.

We open the door,
pull away the blanket.
Two scurry. Three, with coaxing
actually go into the bucket to be released
back into the wild.

Reluctantly, we set wooden traps
baited with peanut butter.
Our task here complete,
we head back to our work, painting and sculpting,

but on the path, a fawn
so small I could pick her up,
her eyes like those of the mice.

Go find the ones we set free, I say.
Tell them not to come back.

She bursts into the air
all feathered tail and spots,
looks over her shoulder once

and with two gambols
becomes only a streak in the tall grass.

Then the mockingbird I've heard all morning
lands on a branch over my head,
her song pitch-perfect for this bright day.

Astonished, Elizabeth, Marcus, and I Stand, and Watch

Sun-warmed air ripples across the aspens
like the angel
troubling
water,

leaves
shiver into
a thousand mirrors

but the breeze meanders on   then so do we.

I Have Always Dreamed of a Meadow

A streak of gold at dawn, it opens
with red-winged blackbirds perched
on swaying milkweed stalks
singing loud hosannas, kong-ka-ree.

Goldenrod waves prayer flags along
the path through the grass
in seven shades of yellow.

At the top of the meadow,
billowing oak, cherry, and maple,
open to a billowing sky

and in the clouds, faeries
and storybook people dance a roundelay,
ladies in conical hats and jousting knights,

> knights like Pammy Lane painted
> in the stairwell of her house
> when we were in fourth grade . . .

children from my *Child's Garden of Verses*
ringed in hollyhocks,
the girl on a swing,
> a child crying . . . .

Eight Dyslexic Kids Before Dyslexia Had a Name

Neither leisure foreigner
caught their heifer
on the weird heights . . .
exceptions to the rule
just as we were.

Bulle*t*in: Bull*et* out.
There is *a rat* in sep*arat*e,
Pap*er*'s from the station*er*y,
and the princip*al* is our p*al*.

Holding aloft imaginary oars,
we sailed across the classroom
from Denmark to England
drinking homemade mead,

danced Ponce de Leon's fountain,
choreographed Balboa's peaceful ocean,

and when Miss Allen held high
Giotto's *Flight to Egypt,* in a wink
we became Mary and Joseph,

the donkey, three trees growing by the road,
a jagged rock, and of course, the angel pointing the way

to that country we would study
in fourth grade and learn to spell
by calling it *E-gee-why-pee-tee.*

We read Marguerite de Angeli's *The Door in the Wall,*
and, as class scribe, I penned a letter to her using
black ink that stained my fingers

then, in pure gold, illuminated
the introductory capital
. . . not a building with a dome.

Already Half a Century

It appears as clouds
over my neighbor's pasture

and among the Black-eyed Susans
on the roadside
between Linville and Pineola.

I learned of Queen Anne's lace
the summer I was twelve,
allowed
for the first time

to have the tiny back bedroom
at my grandmother's house
all to myself.

I woke each morning
in sweltering Georgia heat
and started reading . . .

words on the page described
a lace
with a queen's name
covering the meadow my heroine ran through.

That image still held in my mind
when, years later, I moved to North Carolina,
and saw it
floating in the fields . . .
and that already half a century ago.

Flame

1.

Behind my grandmother's barn,
out past the schoolyard
and beyond old Harvey Stewart's land,
I watched one field after another
burst into flame.

2.

We walked the curved road,
my best friend and I,
until we came to a graveyard
overgrown with lily-of-the-valley,
white flowers spreading like wildfire.

3.

Now, in the blazing meadow
Elizabeth, Blevyn and I
stand transfigured
as we listen to the liquid flute
of the wood thrush.

Waking to Thunder

Two hummingbirds shift up and down
daring each other to sip
the last sweet syrup.

Labor Day comes late this year, though not late enough for me.
A Common Buckeye's cocoa-colored wings
stretched on dead rudbeckias

and the delphinium's last purple plume:
I am desolate.

How lovely it was to wake to thunder
but this evening has turned cool,
the woods silhouette against a burnished sky.

Not willing to go inside where darkness fills the corners,
I wait for vermilion to fade into pearl,
longing to take one last sip.

A Paper Heart

On the dogwood, one red leaf
twirls like a heart cut from paper
and pinned to a twig.

Below, small whirlwinds
uncover a patch of emerald.

I kneel down,
put my cheek to it

and wish for a little girl.

We'd find a hollow stump
and make a fairy house
roofed with moss,

set a toadstool table
with ferns and rosy berries

then press a pathway to the door
with leaves bright and breakable
as my heart.

After the Ball

At twenty-two degrees, the leaves simply let go.
Cast by December's canted sun,
their shadows blur across my bedroom wall.

A single one floats left to right, then a maelstrom.

I want to stay wrapped in blankets watching them,
but, obedient even at seventy-five,

I dress and go to an early morning Nutcracker rehearsal
though my part, an aging granny, needs no practice.

To my delight as I arrive, outside the theater
ginkgoes are standing in puddles of yellow,
their leaves brought down by this first frost—

Five young trees like girls after a ball
stretch bare arms to greet the morning,
and step out of their crinolines.

Light for the Blind Horse

Light for the Blind Horse

Awake past four in the morning
I see through the woods,
half a mile away,
the light
left on by my neighbors
to comfort their blind horse.

An Aubade

I long for the light
on the side of my barn,
for rims of gold
around leaves at dawn,
for my shadow cast downhill
as I step out each morning . . .

The day before I left
I walked Elizabeth's fields,
then she and I swam in her pond at dusk,

came home wet and child-like-happy,
the sun's last touch on the high meadow.

Later, fireflies pulsed
as from the porch we watched a full moon rise.
Kaky and Carol, Blevyn: who else was there?

The peonies were in bloom that June, crimson,
and chairs, the blue ones from my kitchen
        plus two green plastic,
still sat in conversation as I drove away at dawn.

The Japanese Cherry

The first spring after her death
      it bloomed during five days of rain.

I didn't care.
      Let the blossoms be washed away.

Didn't mind if the rose bush
      never recovered from harsh cutting back.

Last night, a dense fog,
      and again this morning.

But as it burns off,
      I see white flowers held against the sky

And in the woods,
      ten thousand spiderwebs bright with dew.

Tomorrow, petals will dress my drive,
      but today, I will agree to this brief beauty.

Missed Seeing It

Not wanting to harm the delicate dunes,
every day for a week, my whole family,
minus one,

walked around the end of the island
where fishermen threw their lines into the inlet.
The way was tedious, chairs cumbersome.

Slopping and loose, the sand burned our feet.
We reached the beach on wobbly legs,
already tired.

But undaunted, we swam
and sunned and people watched,
then trudged the long way home for lunch.

All the while a path lay right in front of us,
a narrow boardwalk through tall spartina grass.
I saw it as we packed to leave for home.

While her children hosed their feet one last time,
I followed it far enough to glimpse the sea
then trying to comfort myself, promised
we'd come back next year . . .

Instructions for Studying Grief in Solitude

Touch toes twice.
Balance on one foot.
Balance on the other.

Follow a trail into the woods
where bogs of bracken
capture then offer back
deep pools of sun.

Rest on claw-like root of the beech tree
in air colored by its leaves
as if by Tiffany glass.

Bathe in columns of light
pouring through balsam, spruce, and fir,
that carry particles of everyone you've loved and lost.

Come once a year to this lambent place,
watch morning fog lift
to reveal the lake's perfect inverse world.

But beware of wind-whipped days
when the lake turns steel
and those restless companions,
fear and anger, intrude.

A Letter from the Mountains to my Dead Parents

It's cold and wet here today not unlike
those few rainy days, the one or two
out of the whole month we always had,
       all of us together.

If it did rain, we worked puzzles.
You, father, hid a piece in your pocket
so you could put in the last one.   Remember?

I loved the pocked surface of the lake,
the smell of wet woods. I walked
along the river so far I sometimes scared myself,

more afraid you'd miss me than I'd be lost.
I was a teen and you were stern
   but you always made me laugh.

And because it was cold, mother, you made me stay in
when I wanted to sail with the boys
as though I had become breakable.

I walk that river now on a trail blazed with blue,
a trail that sixty years ago I thought I discovered.

The fractured water falls from Big Moose to Darts,
trees shred the light

and I allow myself to miss you today.
I weave through the damp morning,
singing to myself.

I did that when I was a child.   Remember?
I sing, Yea though I walk through the valley of the shadow . . .
I sing, Surely *this* is the house of the Lord.

If Only for a Moment

This morning a lark sings somewhere nearby
        telling me to count each day

until I learn that's all I have

and even time filled with nothing
        cannot call it back.

I awoke thinking
        I was in my childhood bed

the whole summer stretched before me
        and all this yet to be.

About the Author

Lynne Santy Tanner was born in New York City where she attended The Chapin School. She graduated from Hollins College, Roanoke, Virginia, with a Bachelor of Arts in Biology and a minor in Dance. She has served as choreographer for the Rutherford County Arts Council for fifty years. Her poetry has been published by Finishing Line Press, Kakalak, QuillsEdge, and Hermit Feathers Press. She lives in Rutherfordton, North Carolina.

www.ingramcontent.com/pod-product-compliance
Lightning Source LLC
Chambersburg PA
CBHW031155090426
42738CB00008B/1340